7530 5267

 **W9-BZA-320**

Why It Matters
Elections

John Son

Children's Press®
An Imprint of Scholastic Inc.

Content Consultant
Saikrishna Bangalore Prakash
James Monroe Distinguished Professor of Law
Paul G. Mahoney Research Professor of Law
Miller Center Senior Fellow
University of Virginia
Charlottesville, Virginia

Teacher Adviser
Rachel Hsieh

Library of Congress Cataloging-in-Publication Data
Names: Son, John, author.
Title: Elections / John Son.
Description: New York : Children's Press, an Imprint of Scholastic, Inc., 2020. | Series: A true book. Why it matters | Includes bibliographical references and index.
Identifiers: LCCN 2019004801| ISBN 9780531231845 (library binding) | ISBN 9780531239964 (pbk.)
Subjects: LCSH: Elections—United States--Juvenile literature.
Classification: LCC JK1978 .S66 2020 | DDC 324.60973—dc23
LC record available at https://lccn.loc.gov/2019004801

All rights reserved. Published in 2020 by Children's Press, an imprint of Scholastic Inc.
Printed in North Mankato, MN, USA 113

SCHOLASTIC, CHILDREN'S PRESS, A TRUE BOOK™, and associated logos are trademarks and/or registered trademarks of Scholastic Inc.

Scholastic Inc., 557 Broadway, New York, NY 10012

1 2 3 4 5 6 7 8 9 10 R 29 28 27 26 25 24 23 22 21 20

Front cover: A young girl with a U.S. flag
Back cover: An "I Voted" sticker

Find the Truth!

Everything you are about to read is true *except* for one of the sentences on this page.

Which one is **TRUE**?

T or F   The voting age changed from 21 years to 18 years during the Civil War.

T or F   The president is elected every four years.

Find the answers in this book.

3

Contents

The BIG Truth

Right or Requirement?

Yo Voté 我已投票 투표했습니다 Burnoto Ako
Я ПРОГОЛОСОВАЛ
मैंने मतदान किया 投票しました
ข้าพเจ้าออกเสียงลงคะแนนแล้ว
Tôi Đã Đi Bầu

I VOTED

People often receive a sticker after they vote.

4

A representative delivers a speech

4 Yes, We Can Vote!

How have voting rights expanded
through the years? **35**

In most states, women voted for the first time in 1920.

Think About It!

Take a close look at the people in this photo. The adults are members of the U.S. Congress. They have all been elected by citizens of the United States to make decisions for them in the government. Their right hands are raised to swear an oath, or promise, to represent your interests to the best of their abilities. The future of our country is in their hands. Do you know how they were elected? Can anyone be elected? Why do elections matter to you?

Intrigued?
Want to know more? Turn the page!

Mayors are elected to help run a city or town. Annise Parker (right) was one of the first openly gay mayors of a major U.S. city. Voters elected her mayor of Houston, Texas, three times.

Free and Fair

Imagine if there were no traffic lights. Or if there were a fire in the school cafeteria and no one came to put it out. What if no one picked up the garbage outside? Thankfully, there are people in the government whose job it is to make sure these tasks are done. They are hired through a process called an election.

Five rules help keep elections free and fair. First, **candidates** must be free to communicate with voters through speeches, meetings, posters, and other methods. Second, no one can be kept from running for an office if he or she meets the job's minimum requirements. Third, people who meet all voting requirements must be allowed to vote. Fourth, people must be able to vote in private. This way, fear or threats will not influence their choices. Fifth, votes must be accurately and fairly counted.

A high school student in Colorado casts her vote for the first time.

These people have visited a polling place to cast their votes.

All states use secret **ballots**. No one can see how another person voted.

The Power of Elections

The United States is a **democracy**. That means Americans choose the people who run the government by voting for them in elections. Any citizen of the United States who is at least 18 years old can register to vote. Once registered, a citizen can vote in any election. Each citizen has one vote. But even if you are not old enough to vote, you can still make a difference in elections by speaking up and volunteering. All Americans, young and old, can do this!

The Limits of Power

Elections motivate our leaders to do their jobs well. If voters aren't pleased with a leader, they can vote for someone else in the next election. Many elected officials have term limits to keep them from becoming too powerful. For example, a president can only be elected twice.

The delegates who wrote the U.S. Constitution created three branches of government. Each branch limits the power of the others.

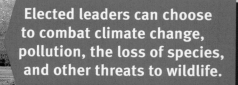

Elected leaders can choose to combat climate change, pollution, the loss of species, and other threats to wildlife.

The Three Branches of Government

Each branch limits the power of the others in a system of checks and balances.

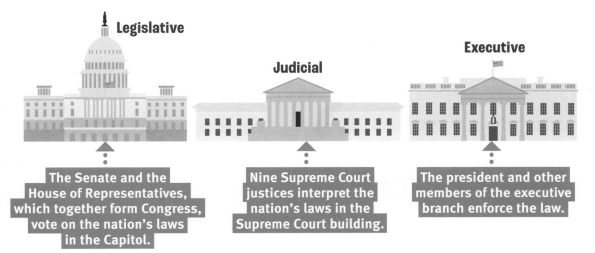

Legislative

Judicial

Executive

The Senate and the House of Representatives, which together form Congress, vote on the nation's laws in the Capitol.

Nine Supreme Court justices interpret the nation's laws in the Supreme Court building.

The president and other members of the executive branch enforce the law.

The Branches of Government

Each of the three branches has a different job. The legislative branch creates laws. It is made up of the Senate and the House of Representatives, together called Congress. The judicial branch interprets those laws. It includes the Supreme Court and other **federal** courts. The executive branch, led by the president, enforces the laws.

There are more than 90,000 state and local governments in the United States.

President Ronald Reagan and his wife, Nancy, wave during the inaugural parade in 1981.

Who Is Elected?

Voters elect officials at three levels: local, state, and federal. Local elections determine a town's council members—the legislative branch. The mayor, who heads the local executive branch, is also elected. In some places, people vote on local judges. At the state level, voters elect the state legislature, the governor, and sometimes state judges. In federal elections, people vote on U.S. congresspeople and the president. The president, acting with the Senate, chooses all federal judges.

Why Do Elections Matter?

Americans participate in the government through elections, and every vote can impact generations. Voters influence your education, what medical services are available, and the taxes people pay. They affect how we treat land and wildlife across the country, and even who can vote in the future! You can see the effects of voter decisions in action. Are the roads in your neighborhood smooth and clear? Do crossing guards help you get to school?

"Another 'undecided.'"

This cartoon shows that deciding who to vote for is not always an easy choice. How would you decide who to vote for?

It's a Big Job

Elected leaders have many, many responsibilities. Local governments run schools, libraries, parks, and local buses and trains. They are also in charge of people you see in emergencies, including police officers, firefighters, and emergency medical workers. Streets, the water supply, and other basics are local, too. State and the federal governments create and enforce laws at their levels. Their decisions can affect education, health, and other services at their level and the local level.

Mayor of New York Bill de Blasio visits a school in 2014.

Who Takes Care of What?

Each of the country's three levels of government has many jobs with many responsibilities.

This diagram shows some of the tasks each level takes care of separately and together.

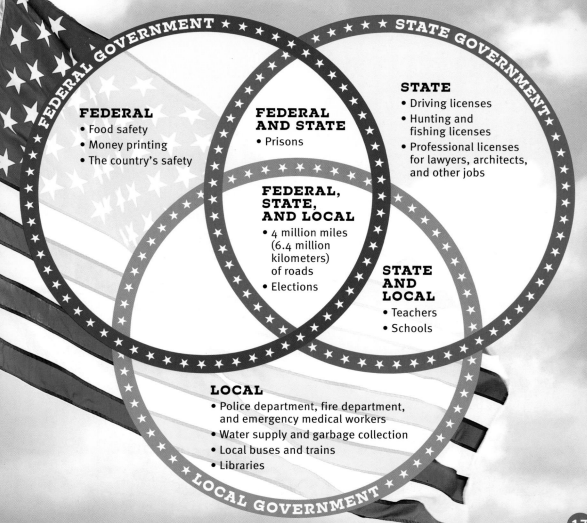

FEDERAL GOVERNMENT

STATE GOVERNMENT

FEDERAL
- Food safety
- Money printing
- The country's safety

FEDERAL AND STATE
- Prisons

STATE
- Driving licenses
- Hunting and fishing licenses
- Professional licenses for lawyers, architects, and other jobs

FEDERAL, STATE, AND LOCAL
- 4 million miles (6.4 million kilometers) of roads
- Elections

STATE AND LOCAL
- Teachers
- Schools

LOCAL
- Police department, fire department, and emergency medical workers
- Water supply and garbage collection
- Local buses and trains
- Libraries

LOCAL GOVERNMENT

Missouri U.S. Senate candidate Josh Hawley greets supporters as he arrives to cast his vote on election day in 2018.

The first woman to run for president was Victoria Woodhull in 1872.

CHAPTER

Running for Office

Do you want to run for a government office someday? Candidates for all jobs must be U.S. citizens. Most offices have age requirements too. According to the Constitution, a person must be at least 35 years old to be president or vice president. A senator must be 30, and a representative must be 25. Once a person decides to run for office, no matter what level of government, it takes months of hard work and the help of many dedicated people to win.

Artists often use a donkey to stand for the Democratic Party and an elephant for the Republican Party. In this cartoon, both political parties are squeezing the nation, represented by Uncle Sam. What do you think this cartoon is trying to say?

Time to Party

Candidates generally belong to a political party. A party is a group of people who support a similar approach to government. The United States has two main parties: Democratic and Republican. Both parties agree on many national goals but often disagree on how to reach those goals.

Candidates may be members of other, smaller parties, such as the Green and Independent Parties.

On the Campaign Trail

Every candidate **campaigns**, particularly presidential candidates. Candidates must raise money to print signs, run TV commercials, and pay many of the hardworking people helping them. They also organize and travel to rallies and speeches in dozens of towns and cities.

An important part of a campaign is creating a slogan. This is a short, catchy saying that can help voters remember candidates and what they stand for.

SLOGAN	CANDIDATE
"Happy Days Are Here Again" (1936)	Franklin D. Roosevelt
"I Like Ike" (1952)	Dwight D. Eisenhower
"Not Just Peanuts" (1976)	Jimmy Carter
"Change We Can Believe In" (2008)	Barack Obama
"Make America Great Again" (2016)	Donald Trump

Some experts believe a memorable slogan can help win an election. Here are a few examples from past presidential campaigns.

Winning the Primaries

Several candidates can run for a party's nomination. Each party can **nominate** only one candidate per election. Parties choose their candidate through primaries or caucuses. In primaries, voters simply cast ballots. In a caucus, however, voters give or listen to speeches, participate in debates, and then vote. Each party selects a nominee based on who wins those elections. A presidential nominee announces a running mate, who would become vice president if the candidate won.

Supporting a Candidate

Individuals can give their own money to support or work against a candidate. But over the years, laws made it illegal for companies and **unions** to do so. In 2008, an organization called Citizens United wanted to release a film against candidate Hillary Clinton. Money from companies had helped make the film, which was illegal at the time. In 2010, the Supreme Court ruled on the case *Citizens United v. Federal Election Commission*. The justices decided that the donation laws in place partly went against the freedom of speech. Since then, anyone can donate to an independent commercial, film, or other product for or against a candidate. All independent products have to publicly list all the people and groups that donated to it. Companies are still banned from donating directly to a candidate.

The Supreme Court building

Presidential nominees Donald Trump and Hillary Clinton hold their final televised debate before the election in 2016.

About 84 million people watched the first presidential debate between Trump and Clinton in 2016, more than any other televised debate in U.S. history.

Who Will Be Elected?

The weeks leading up to Election Day are extra busy, filled with rallies and speeches and cheering crowds. Meanwhile, you and all Americans can learn about the candidates and the issues on the ballot. You can read newspapers and voting guides, and watch live debates between the candidates. It's also important for you to talk with people who have similar opinions to yours as well as those who disagree.

When Are Elections Held?

Americans choose their president every four years on the first Tuesday after November 1. Some states choose their representatives for Congress at the same time. People vote on other federal offices during another national election two years later, halfway through a president's term.

Each state decides when to elect its governor, state legislators, and other state officers. There are also county, city, and school board elections at various times.

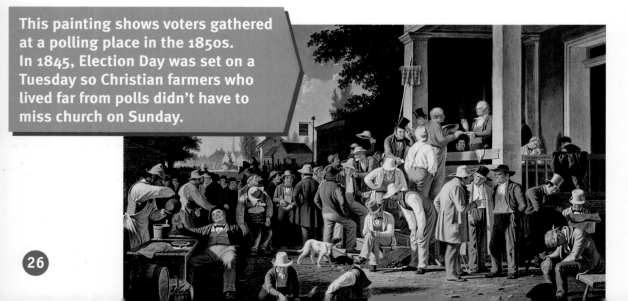

This painting shows voters gathered at a polling place in the 1850s. In 1845, Election Day was set on a Tuesday so Christian farmers who lived far from polls didn't have to miss church on Sunday.

Voter Registration

Anyone who wants to vote must first register as a voter. If you don't register, you can't vote! In most states, voters are automatically registered when they get a driver's license. But what if you live elsewhere, or you don't drive? To make registration easier for everyone, some states allow voters to register right at a polling place on Election Day. Online registration is common too. There are also voter registration drives, when volunteers remind the public to register and provide any needed paperwork.

This cartoon seems to say it doesn't matter *what* candidates say as much as *how* they say it. Do you think this is true?

In some states, all elections are done with ballots that voters mail in.

Polls Are the Place to Be

When Election Day arrives, voters go to polling places, also called polls, to cast their vote. Polling places are usually set up in public buildings such as schools and post offices. Voters are assigned polling places based on where they live. This means a person's poll should never be far from home!

A citizen can only vote once. If someone tries to vote more than once, it is voter fraud. The person could be arrested.

Casting Ballots

Votes are cast on ballots that list the names of candidates. The ballot can include candidates running for president, senator, representative, or governor. It could also list local candidates running for mayor, city council, or school board. Most polls use paper ballots. Voters fill in circles to cast their votes. The votes are then scanned and counted by a machine. Another way to vote is by touching a computer screen or pushing buttons.

Ballots can be printed in many different languages. This makes it possible for anyone to vote, whether they speak English or not.

A person who is out of town on Election Day can still vote by mailing in an absentee ballot.

J. B. Pritzker and his running mate, Juliana Stratton, celebrate their victory as the new governor and lieutenant governor of Illinois on election night in 2018.

Victory Party

In most state and federal elections, candidates win by a plurality. That means the winner must receive more votes than any other candidate. A candidate can often do this without winning a majority, or more than half, of the votes. One major exception is the president, who needs a majority of the electoral votes. Win or lose, candidates thank voters and the people who helped them.

Electoral College

Every vote for a presidential candidate is really a vote for the citizen's state **electors**. Each state has a number of electors equal to the number of legislators it has in the U.S. Congress. The 538 total electors in presidential elections form the electoral college. The winner of the presidential election needs a majority of the electoral votes, or at least 270. A candidate can receive the most individual votes, which is called the popular vote, but still not win enough electors!

In 2000, Al Gore (left) won the popular vote for the presidency. But George W. Bush (right) had more electoral votes, making him the 43rd president. Other presidents who lost the popular vote are John Quincy Adams, Rutherford B. Hayes, Benjamin Harrison, and Donald Trump.

U.S. Electoral Votes by State
(as of 2019)

WA 12
OR 7
MT 3
ND 3
MN 10
ME 4
VT 3
NH 4
MA 11
NY 29
ID 4
WY 3
SD 3
WI 10
MI 16
RI 4
CT 7
NV 6
UT 6
CO 9
NE 5
IA 6
IL 20
IN 11
OH 18
PA 20
NJ 14
DE 3
MD 10
DC 3
CA 55
KS 6
MO 10
KY 8
WV 5
VA 13
AZ 11
NM 5
OK 7
AR 6
TN 11
NC 15
SC 9
MS 6
AL 9
GA 16
TX 34
LA 8
AK 3
HI 4
FL 29

Right or Requirement

For Americans, voting is a right and a responsibility. It is also a choice. No one is required to vote. But in many elections today, not everyone turns up to vote. In recent presidential elections, only about 60 percent of eligible voters actually voted. This percentage is even lower for state and local elections. Some people think citizens should be required to vote. Others argue that it is a citizen's right to choose.

What do you think?

Should Americans be required to vote?

YES	NO
✔ Like paying taxes, voting is a duty that supports the government.	✔ Forcing people to vote violates the freedom of choice guaranteed in the Bill of Rights.
✔ If more people vote, the opinions of the people are more accurately represented in government.	✔ People who are not interested in voting could make careless or random choices.
✔ Making voting a requirement would force people to be better informed about candidates and issues.	✔ Some people may resent and work against a government that requires them to vote.
✔ Fines paid by those who do not vote could help support government activities.	✔ Finding and punishing nonvoters could be expensive and time-consuming.

I VOTED

Yo Voté 我已投票 투표했습니다 Bumoto Ako
Я ПРОГОЛОСОВАЛ បុ សិ្នបោះឆ្នោត ហើយ
मैंने मतदान किया 投票しました ខ្ញុំបានបោះឆ្នោត
ข้าพเจ้าออกเสียงลงคะแนนแล้ว
Tôi Đã Đi Bầu

Texas is the only state that allows American astronauts to vote from space.

George Washington was elected the first president of the United States in 1789. Only about 43,000 people voted. In 2016, almost 130 million people voted!

Yes, We Can Vote!

When the U.S. Constitution was written in 1787, it did not set any rules about voting. It left each state to make up their own voting laws. In the first presidential election in 1789, only about 1 percent of the population had **suffrage**, or could vote. All of them were wealthy white men. The rules in the Constitution, however, allowed it to be changed by adding **amendments**. Over time, amendments and laws have expanded voting rights.

15th Amendment

After the Civil War ended in 1865, all enslaved people were freed. Five years later, states added the 15th Amendment to the Constitution. This made it illegal to prevent African American men from voting. But for almost a century, the amendment had little impact. Officials used methods such as violence and literacy tests to exclude African Americans from voting.

Timeline of U.S. Voting Rights

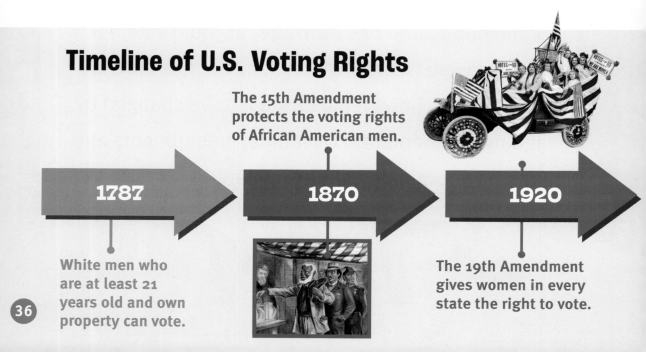

The 15th Amendment protects the voting rights of African American men.

1787

1870

1920

White men who are at least 21 years old and own property can vote.

The 19th Amendment gives women in every state the right to vote.

19th Amendment

Before the 1900s, women could vote in only a few states. To change this, many people took part in marches, meetings, and public speeches. But they did not have support from Congress until World War I (1914–1918). Women took over jobs left by men who had joined the military. After the war, activists used this to convince Congress that women could and should vote. In 1920, the 19th Amendment officially gave women in all states the right to vote.

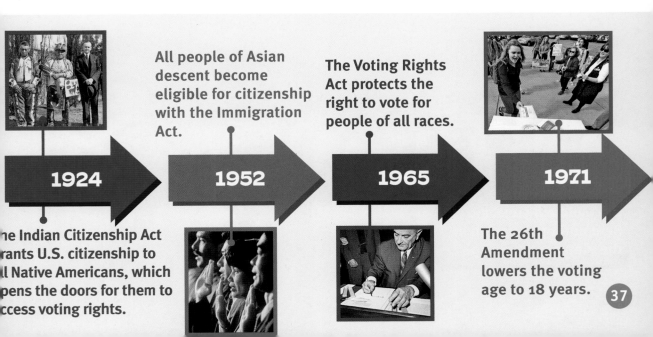

All people of Asian descent become eligible for citizenship with the Immigration Act.

The Voting Rights Act protects the right to vote for people of all races.

1924

1952

1965

1971

he Indian Citizenship Act rants U.S. citizenship to ll Native Americans, which pens the doors for them to ccess voting rights.

The 26th Amendment lowers the voting age to 18 years.

26th Amendment

In the 1960s, the United States was heavily involved in the Vietnam War (1954–1975). Thousands of men as young as 18 years old were being drafted, or forced, into the military. Many young people protested. At the time, citizens had to be 21 years old to vote. People could be drafted before they could vote for or against the politicians sending them to war. The 26th Amendment changed that in 1971, lowering the voting age to 18.

U.S. soldiers cross a field during a mission in the Vietnam War in 1967.

Susan B. Anthony

Susan Brownell Anthony (1820–1906) was a social activist. She fought for a number of causes, such as ending slavery and reforming child labor. She is most remembered for her work on women's suffrage. For 50 years, she led a tireless effort with Elizabeth Cady Stanton to bring equal rights to women. The work was not always easy. They organized demonstrations, gave lectures, and started a regular publication to spread their ideas. In 1872, Anthony was part of a group of women who were arrested and fined for attempting to vote. Anthony's heroic actions eventually paved the way for the 19th Amendment.

Susan B. Anthony

Activists Martin Luther King Jr. (in white hat), Coretta Scott King, and thousands of others marched 54 miles (87 km) to demand voting rights.

Voting Rights Act of 1965

Despite the 15th and 19th Amendments, black Americans often suffered violent voter **suppression** for many years. In March 1965, people organized a march from Selma to Montgomery in Alabama. Participants hoped to bring attention to this and other issues black Americans were facing. It took three tries to complete the march. The first attempt ended in violence from the police. But the marchers succeeded. Congress passed the Voting Rights Act that same year.

Gerrymandering

Voters still face issues. Every state is divided into election districts. District boundaries can be drawn to benefit or hurt a particular community. This is called gerrymandering. For example, a political group might be divided among many districts. This makes it difficult for that group to have a majority anywhere and limits their voice in government.

Americans need elections to help make their voices heard. This is why so many people have fought for free and fair elections since the country was born.

Take a look at this cartoon. Is the "Voting Machine" new or old? Simple? Complex? Does the machine seem reliable? What do you think the cartoon's creator is trying to say about U.S. elections?

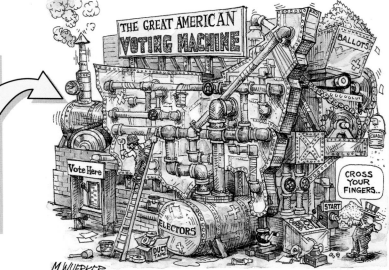

M. WUERKER

POLITICO Universal Uclick

©Matt Wuerker/Distributed by Universal Uclick via CartoonStock.com

Road to Change

Kids aren't old enough to vote or run for office. But kids across the country have still made impacts on candidates and elected officials.

In 2018, survivors of a tragic high school shooting in Parkland, Florida, went on a nationwide bus tour. They named the tour "Road to Change." Their main mission was to motivate young people to vote and be informed. These students encouraged young voters to register, study the issues and candidates, and vote in the 2018 elections. The effort paid off. More young people voted in 2018 than in 2014!

Young people gather to protest and use the hashtag #notonemore on social media posts to voice their support for gun control.

42

Mari Copeny hugs President Obama. Mari, called "Little Miss Flint," continues to raise money and bring awareness about her city to others.

In 2016, eight-year-old Mari Copeny wrote a letter to President Barack Obama. The water in her home of Flint, Michigan, was full of dangerous substances and unsafe to drink. In her letter, Mari asked the president to meet with activists traveling to Washington, D.C., to bring attention to the water crisis. Obama wrote her back, saying that he would visit Flint himself. The events brought national attention to the problem.

Get Involved!

If you're too young to vote, there is still plenty you can do to be an active citizen. Try taking these steps:

Learn about important issues by following the news through multiple sources.

Follow local community leaders online.

Talk with others about the issues. Ask questions to understand their points of view.

Make your voice heard by writing, emailing, or calling local, state, and national leaders.

Did you find the truth?

(F) The voting age changed from 21 years to 18 years during the Civil War.

(T) The president is elected every four years.

Resources

The book you just read is a first introduction to elections, and to the history and government of our country. There is always more to learn and discover. In addition to this title, we encourage you to seek out complementary resources.

Other books in this series:

You can also look at:

Grayson, Robert. *Voters: From Primaries to Decision Night*. Minneapolis: Lerner Publications, 2016.

Gunderson, Jessica. *Understanding Your Role in Elections*. North Mankato, MN: Capstone Press, 2018.

Roosevelt, Eleanor, with Michelle Markel. *When You Grow Up to Vote*. New York: Roaring Book Press, 2018.

Shamir, Ruby, and Matt Faulkner. *What's the Big Deal About Elections*. New York: Philomel Books, 2018.

Glossary

amendments (uh-MEND-muhnts) changes that are made to a law or a legal document

ballots (BAL-uhts) systems of secret voting or papers used to vote

campaigns (kam-PAYNZ) takes organized action to achieve a particular goal, such as winning an election

candidates (KAN-duh-dates) people who are applying for a job or running in an election

democracy (dih-MAH-kruh-see) a form of government in which the people choose their leaders in elections

electors (uh-LEK-torz) people (in the electoral college) who cast their votes based on who the majority of citizens voted for in their state

federal (FED-ur-uhl) national; describing a system of government in which states are united under a central authority

nominate (NAH-muh-nate) to suggest someone for an important job or to receive an honor

suffrage (SUHF-rij) the right to vote

suppression (suh-PRESH-uhn) the act of stopping something, especially by using authority or force

unions (YOON-yuhnz) groups of workers organized to help improve such things as working conditions and wages

Index

Page numbers in **bold** indicate illustrations.

About the Author

John Son is the author of *Finding My Hat*, a New York Public Library Best Book for the Teen Age about his adventures growing up in Texas as a Korean American, and *If You Were a Kid on the Mayflower*. He has also written two other titles in the A True Book series, *Relaxation and Yoga* and *Asia*. He lives with his family in Brooklyn, New York.